I'LL ALWAYS BE FROM LORAIN

Harry Youtt

Second Edition
2016

[1st Edition Pub'd 2006]

DEDICATION and ACKNOWLEDGMENTS

I'm dedicating this collection of verses to everyone who was part of Lorain as it really was, in what were truly the "good old days." Those days were actually not that long ago. There was a spirit to the place in the '40's and 50's and 60's of the last century that lingers even until now. That spirit came from what everybody thought was possible for the town back then. This book is for those who formed that spirit out of their dreams and their hard work.

I published the original edition of this collection in 2006, and back then, I acknowledged the people who originally contributed their support and input to the process. That acknowledgment and appreciation continue. They contributed not only their encouragement and comments but also their own memories to help enhance mine: Nancy Conn Terjesen, Carolyn Sipkovsky, Jeff and Betty (Coats) Smith, Linda Bornstein Stone, and Stan and Nancy Youtt.

The original edition was distributed by what was then the Black River Historical Society and has now become the Lorain Historical Society (www.lorainhistory.org). That organization was the real inspiration-source that got me started and kept me going in writing this collection. It started when I first visited and lost myself among the photos in the archive. Who would ever have imagined there'd be so many pictures of Lorain, all accessible and in the same place? Everything seemed to be calling out to be remembered and noted - right down to the Lorain Creamery milk delivery wagon, intact and bright painted and standing out in the back parking lot, just as if all the clocks were turned back and it was 1947 again!

A LITTLE ABOUT ME

As for me, I graduated from Lorain High School in 1960. Education-wise, it was all downhill from there. Aside from my annual return visits every summer, I've been away from Lorain much longer than the time I actually spent there growing up.

For several summers, I conducted poetry workshops for the Dylan Thomas Society, in the Swansea house where Dylan was born. I speak occasionally, mainly about aspects of creativity and consciousness, and about plain-speech resonance poetry, primarily in Ireland, England and Wales.

Now, in the autumn of my career, I'm still teaching creative writing (27 years!) in the UCLA Extension Writers' Program in California, where I reside. If you want to be in touch, feel free to locate me on Facebook [facebook.com/harry.youtt], or "tweet" me (@HarryYoutt), or even email me at harryyoutt@ucla.edu.

-

TABLE OF CONTENTS

Introduction   1

I. Memory Landmarks

NOW HERE WE ARE	3
I'LL ALWAYS BE FROM LORAIN	3
A CHILD'S CHRISTMAS IN LORAIN	4
LIBRARY IN THE GROVE	11
LIGHTHOUSE	13
LAKEVIEW PARK	16
LAKE THAT CARVED OHIO	18
TORNADO	21
CITY OF PORCHES	22
TRAINS GOING EVERYDAY SOMEWHERE	26

II. Industry that Was

IN THE GRAND OLD BLAST FURNACE DAYS	27
SLAG MOUNTAIN	29
AT NIGHT, THE RIVER	31
BEAM LAUNCH OF THE WILFRED SYKES	32
ORE DOCKS	33
GYPSUM PLANT	34
STEEL PLANT TOUR	36
BUT IT WASN'T ONLY THE STEEL	37

III. Sundry Places

FIRST CONGREGATIONAL CHURCH	38
THE TRAIN STATION	39
BROADWAY BUILDING	41
ANTLERS HOTEL	42
THE CIVIL DEFENSE TOWER	43
THE HIGH SCHOOL	44

IV. War and Remembrance

THE UNION SOLDIER STATUE	48

FLAG MAST AT THE NAVAL RESERVE	49
HEROES OF THE TWO BRIDGES	51

V. Seasons

THE SUMMER CIRCUS COMES TO TOWN IN DEAD OF NIGHT	54
LAKE FLIES	55
OCTOBER LEAVES	56
SOMETIMES THE SNOW	57
EASTER	58

VI. Eatery

CHOCOLATE SODAS	60
SUTTER'S RESTAURANT	62
FISH FRY AT THE MOOSE HALL	63
HEILMAN'S RESTAURANT	64
MR. GOULD'S CORNER STORE	66

VII. Some People

STANLEY DAVIES AT THE DAIRY QUEEN	68
LEARNING TO SWIM IN LORAIN	70
THE HIGH SCHOOL HIRES A NEW GUY	71
OUT AT THE OLD AIRPORT	72
WILD WEST	73
MILK WAGON	75
DUCK BLINDS	76

VIII. Late Words

WHEN I WAS A BOY	77
IT IS EARLY STILL AND YOU HAVE NEVER FLOWN	78
THE THINGS THAT MADE THE TOWN CLASSY	80
NOW HERE WE ARE (reprise)	82

INTRODUCTION

I grew up in Lorain. I've been away for a lot more than 40 years, but still I know that I'll always be from Lorain. I'm proud of that.

I call these Memory Verses. Maybe I should refer to the whole process as Versified Memory – and leave it at that.

It's like the good old <u>Spoon River Anthology</u> except the people in it aren't coming from their graves and talking about the lives they once led. My people are alive in my head and living in my good old days, just going on with their lives indefinitely. I'm pretty sure that was the way it was for Edgar Lee Masters and his Spoon River people too. It isn't only the people for me; it's the places themselves. So that even if you've never been in my town, that doesn't matter. It's the feelings I'm hoping you'll get that will make it fascinating for you. The good parts of nostalgia. I'm hoping this will trigger your own memories, wherever you come from, so that you'll remember to appreciate the beauty and fondness you carry with you at least about some parts of your own separate pasts. Of course it will help if you're actually from Lorain yourself, or from the Midwest, but I'm guessing it will even be very similar if you're coming from New England, or the South, or the Rockies or the Far West. Maybe even other parts of the world. Just about everybody will always be from somewhere. The emotions and the positive experiences of nostalgia provide a sort of universality that bonds us. We all are a lot more alike than some people would try to have us believe.

If something like this happens for you when you read these, I'll be happy. It's what I'm hoping will happen. It's the reason I decided to make the collection available beyond those of my home town people who've been able to read the original edition locally since 2006.

Yes, these verses do qualify as poetry. But unlike a lot of contemporary trends in modern poetry, these are all accessible and as fully understandable as I can make them. Nothing is obscure. And for me, it's the verse form that unlocks them. Some of them stretch out to be stories. Others sometimes tail into reveries. At one point, for example, I even imagined dwelling and raising a family in the old lighthouse!

*There's a purpose to poetry that goes beyond the simple
collection of words. To be anything, it has to accomplish
discoveries beyond the dazzle of the page it's written on. I
break the lines the way I do so you can get some idea of the
way my mind breathes when the words come to me. I find that
when I do this, I pay better attention to the shapes of the
phrasing I use along the way, as I describe the images I
remember. The whole experience has helped to bring
everything back, after a long time away.*

*If it makes sense to you, I suggest you read these one at a
time. Savor them for what they are. Read them aloud maybe.
They'll take you back to where it all happened, even if you
were never actually there yourself. They take me back when I
read them now.*

*After the long Christmas poem and the first few of my
memory landmarks, I've loosely organized most of the verses
into topical sections: industry, especially the steel that was
always the leading character of the drama that was Lorain back
then, places I remember, seasons, food, people, war and
remembrance. Sometimes these categories really aren't that
tight. You might just want to scroll through the titles in the
Table of Contents and find something you like. Or you can just
flip the book open to anywhere and take potluck. It isn't that
big anyway.*

*I haven't tried to set down my whole history, and I can't
even say this little collection sets out the best of everything
that happened to me. It's just the stuff that came out to set
itself down when I summoned it.*

*I hope that reading these verses reminds you of your own
reasons to be proud of a town that was magnificent in its day,
a town that can even be magnificent again.*

I. Memory Landmarks

NOW HERE WE ARE

Now here we are, full formed,
out beyond the sperm and the egg
spark-forged in the dark,
and sprung into our own generation.
Looking back through the dim night
to the tiny lights of the place that spawned us.
Trying to find a pattern,
trying to see what it means.

I'LL ALWAYS BE FROM LORAIN

No matter how far I've gone away, I'll always be from Lorain.
I carry this on my back like a dusty tortoise shell.
I duck beneath it, and it shelters me.
Whenever someone comes and thumps it,
I hear that echo, and remember who I really am.

I could have come from one of those bedroom suburbs
with a thump-less, echo-less name
on the fringe of some tedious metropolis,
where nothing really ever happens
and the skies are never orange with possibility.
But Lorain! The name swirls up – cyclone of dry leaves
on a windy and unsettled day --
memories fluttering down all over the place!
No matter how far I've gone away, I'll always be from Lorain.

To get things started, here is my fond memory of Christmas in the good old days, snowballed into one big outburst of words. Christmas was the town's BIG holiday when I was a boy, probably still is, and it always brought out the best of the town, so it's a good place to begin.

For awhile I used to lead poetry workshops for Welsh poets in Swansea Wales, in the house where Dylan Thomas lived as a boy, in the very room where he was born. Dylan of course had long ago written "A Child's Christmas in Wales" about his own Swansea memories. I'd walk around the rooms of the house late at night. I'd walk all over Swansea and visit the places he'd written about in his Christmas story. Maybe that was what got me started. I don't know. Maybe it was the encouraging Christmas spirit of the Poet himself. But it got me to thinking, maybe I should write my own "Child's Christmas" and take down what I remember.

So here it is, with cheers for the season. I'll be happy if you read it to remember. Read it to find what used to be, and compare it with what is now. Read it to your kids and your grandkids at Christmas, by the glow of a fireplace, maybe, to keep the spirit going.

A CHILD'S CHRISTMAS IN LORAIN

This is just the way it was, and in my deep heart,
this is the way it always will be Christmas
in the twinkling Harbor Town
at the south edge of the ice-lake
that by December was always
just about to be freezing solid.
And the Lake seemed already angry
the winter hadn't fully descended yet,
to cast aside any gestures at festivity,
ice chunks hissing together
and rolling gray water surge.
But the town would never freeze,
even when the lake fought hard
and the winds tried to blow the candles out.

It would snow sometimes, oh yes, it would
sometimes be snowing through December,
as colored lights were strung along perimeters of houses,
and plywood silhouettes of reindeer were trundled out
to front lawns and spotlighted for passers-by to see.

The stores would start putting out their signs:
"Open til 9 every nite before Xmas,"
and Broadway would deck across itself
with swaying bell-shaped lights, three red ones in a row,
string after string as the avenue curved south,
with each bell of a string lighting in sequence,
first the left angled one, then the center, then the right,
as if lights could reveal a semblance of tolling.
And children, first ones to be delighted by the season,
would snuggle into back seats of family cars
and count the number of times they could
see the bells of a string light up, all across,
before they passed by beneath it.

To the sounds of crunching snow
beneath trudging booted shopper-feet
wending down a semi-shoveled Broadway after dark,
add the jingling hand-bells, wrung constant
over tri-podded pots with mesh covers
and holes big enough for quarters and half dollars.

Courtesy of some enterprising merchant or other,
you could hear scratchy phonographed Christmas music
piped outside and onto the street.
Sometimes you could even listen to a rag-tag
Salvation Army band, gathered at the corner of
6th Street or mid-block in front of the Kresge's Dime Store,
coronet and baritone horn and
maybe even a dented tuba, burnished silver,

in the hands of its earnest over-coated owner,
playing *Gloria in Excelces Deo* along with everybody else,
and they somehow managed to end up
at the final *Deo* together, with every once in a while
the booming sound of a 'Ho-ho-ho'
from a wandering Santa down the street,
bending to bestow cellophane covered candy canes
upon children -- who were dazzled by the honor of it all.

At the J.C. Penney Store, parents would
make their purchases of "sensible" gifts
that children would be least excited to open:
balled socks and plaid shirts, belts and
sometimes a billfold, mittens, knitted caps,
and dungarees lined with flannel,
while above the Penney fray, money, placed into
brass canisters would zing and catapult on rope chords
that were strung across the ceiling
up to a single sensible cashier
who'd make change and catapult it
back down the line, while the 'sensible' gifts
were wrapped in tissue and boxed
by 'sensible' clerks -- anxious for the season to be over.

Every family would choose a night
in the time before *The Big Day,* for a slow drive
street-by-street around the neighborhoods
to gaze at the light displays:
spotlighted sleighs on rooftops, with cut-out reindeer
and *Rudolfs* blinking obligatory red noses.
Sprays of lights that fastened to the sides of houses
and made the night seem almost bright as day,
multicolored of course but hundreds and hundreds
of bulbs that splashed light out upon snow
and even up at the stars.

Only the moon could reign against such light
on nights when the storms were down.
And in the windows of a single house
in which an aging lady lived alone –
candles, real candles, one to a window
upstairs and downstairs, flickering in that
unmistakable way that only flamed candles can flicker.
A few people would stop to linger at the Candle House.
Silence would hold them there
and link them to other silent seekers.

On one snow-crunching evening
during those days when time seemed
to be grinding to some kind of standstill,
over at the high school, green-robed choristers
with silver-satin sashes flapping,
would step forward, one by one, singing
'Come all ye Faithful' down rickety aisles
and up onto the auditorium stage.
Each of them as they marched
would be holding a single electrified white candlestick,
turned on by twisting the flame-bulb
just before the procession began.
And festive friends and family would be
scrunched into seats and smiling, so that ever after,
everyone who sang those words, in their minds would see
those wobble-marching candles
and wonder at the brightness of winter memory.

Caroling then, on Christmas Eve, up and down
the neighborhood streets. Clustered families,
everybody woolen-coated and mufflered,
snow suited and knit capped,
and semi-circling houses of unsuspecting shut-ins,
to give them a choral show the likes of which
they hadn't seen since last year.
Of course there would be cookies, from tins,

and occasional eggnog for grown-ups.

Lights of the midnight-services churches
warming the dark wooden panels of walls,
making them different places than the morning churches
everyone had gotten used to.
Candles everywhere and doing real work
the way candles once did long ago,
and the rosy-gleamy faces of the hymn-singers
smiles back and forth in the spirit of things,
Hark the herald, Joy to the World and *Sing choirs of angels,*
the organ booming and the hung ropes of evergreen
seeming to sway in the music of it all,
One of the elder men wearing a plaid vest and a red bow tie
would read from the scripture-pulpit,
in a booming voice nobody ever knew that he had:
"Fear not, for behold I bring you good tidings of great joy."
In the balcony a trio of trumpeters-- suddenly sounding forth
and startling everybody into ecstasy.

Afterwards, crunching through cold snow,
people would be laughing and shouting Merry Christmas
to each other, as if anyone had to be reminded.

Christmas Day would dawn crisp, and
with sunshine sometimes, but probably only gray,
except, this day it wouldn't be bleak,
and there'd be a clear snap to the cold,
with snow that fell two days ago,
having stayed miraculously white.
Green leaves of holly circled into a
thick-prickly wreath hanging on the front door.
And the sun coming out surprised itself –
shining down on everything
and glistening the clanging steeple bells
in the churches all over the town.

Inevitably there would be sleds on Christmas morning
a new one for a younger sibling of course
because the oldest kid would have been handed down
the weathered one, wood-darkened by long years in garages
and always just a little bit sturdier,
taken down from its spike and hauled out
whenever the snow fell.
But the new one would be leaning against
the Christmas tree wall and wrapped round
with a wide red shiny ribbon and bow.
After the toys had been wrestled from wrappings,
and wrappings crumpled and wadded away,
the dinner was put on to roast in slow ovens.

It was then that the streets would fill
with steamy-breath kids in their brand new
'sensible' mittens, red, and green, and the wool still stiff.
The side streets were always plowed after snowfall,
not salted, and the snow surface packed hard
for running in rubber boots and belly-flopping
down onto old sleds and new sibling-sleds
with steel runners hissing,
sliding in rills car tires had made.
Ropes pulled by parents or the bigger kids
would whisk the littlest children along behind,
as they held on tight, reveling in the glory
of being outside and included in the grand festivities.

In the later afternoon, back inside
the steamy-windowed houses,
everybody ruddy faced and sitting at the table
trimmed in red with holly-circled candlesticks,
and for everyone a square of green Jell-O
set upon a single leaf of iceberg lettuce.
Sliced turkey breast, drumsticks and wings,

oyster dressing, a china bowl heaped with mashed potatoes,
everybody festive, and kids bouncing in their chairs
and then scrambling off before pumpkin pie
to run electric trains in circles 'round the Christmas tree.
Grandfathers would follow soon, and creaking their knees
down to train level, they'd be giving engineer advice
to get the tracks laid and the trains running.

As the sun disappeared from the low sky,
and the windows darkened on the day,
fires would crackle in marble-faced fireplaces,
gently roasting the surfaces of teenagers
who drowsed on carpets.

At the very end of the day,
sitting at the window end of beds, gazing out
over snow lawns and up to the sky,
we'd finally remember to search for that
single star that started it all,
wishing it might have returned
to give everybody the new hope they might need
to get us all through another year.

For a moment someone would be certain
the Star had been found, bright and crystal clear.
Yes! Right there!
Then the Season's visions would begin slowly to blur,
as eyes would fall shut,
and under the heavy woolen blankets,
Christmas memories would begin
to dwindle down into dreams.

There was only one library in Lorain back at the beginning of my memory. It has now become The Lorain Historical Society. The branches came later. And there it stands, that little building in the park on 10th Street, near the tracks. It is still such a magnificent place of magic -- clearly the birthplace of my own creative rumblings. And so, I've placed this poem right up among the early ones in this collection.

LIBRARY IN THE GROVE

Midst a darker grove of trees in that city of darker groves,
and the long lawn between the trees
criss-crossed by dim-lighted pathways at night,
and standing alone in the sharp blue darkness
-- the old brick Carnegie library,
window-lighted on both of its floors
when things inside were active.

The boy was certain that down in the dark of the grove,
Arthur and his Round Table Knights were dreaming,
sleeping their long sleep until they were needed,
huddled against each other for warmth
and concealed inside a deep clay cave
scooped from under the flourishing roots of the tallest Ash tree.

They awaited only a signal to action,
the almost-whispered call of that tiny, story-telling librarian
whose passion in this life it always was
to enrapture children's minds,
infuse them with possibilities that always
burst upward from imagination's universal mantra:

"Once upon a time . . .!"
 Hearing this quiet proclamation drift out
through a slightly opened window
of the story room upstairs,

a single groved horse would whinny,
tentative at first, as if clearing its deep throat,
and then another horse would answer, and another.
Hooves would stomp, and crackled leaves would rustle;
shields and swords and armor would clank,
and then hoof beats would suddenly gallop Arthur and his men
across the grove, with only shadows of them visible
in low light from street lamps.

With a rush and a rumble, in they would burst
through the double doors, onto the first floor,
scattering tattered runner-rugs and
almost upsetting the glassed arrays of new books,
and then, clattering up the rickety wooden staircase
 -- and into the story room to greet the floored circle of
open-mouthed children, whose faces never flinched.

Nobody from the reading room or even from the stacks
would ever even think to try and shush them.

Now fifty, no, nearly sixty years later
the mouth of the boy inside the man-grown-old
but never grown too old for new stories, or old stories,
hangs open, at the vision of that grand and dark
birthday cake of a library building
in the middle of that darker grove,
and Arthur and his Knights, roused from their long sleep,
pounding through the magic all around.
And in the center of every possibility,
always that tiny librarian.

LIGHTHOUSE
(for Wayne Conn, who knew from the beginning it couldn't be allowed to disappear)

The lighthouse anchors the town of Lorain, always,
built as if it were the home of some eccentric family,
content to live a life apart, and guard against
marauding monsters from the sea.
Lighthouse - mainstay of the city's definition.

Solid, it looks to be carved out of rock,
rising three stories above its over-thick base,
the last place you'd ever think would disappear,
even in a perfect storm.

Peaked red roof, even a brick chimney,
and of course, that Fresnel lantern cylinder,
set into that high railed walk atop the tower,
looking almost like the steeple on a chapel,
circling bright beam of beacon light
once every thirty seconds,
telling the world where to find us
from out of the dark.

Foghorn dormer, and big windows everywhere,
even up the tower, even an attic window,
just under the peak,
each framed by massive steel shutters
that really mean business when the going gets rough.
Davits and rails and gangways.

As a boy I dreamed of bringing my new family back
to live out there, my pretty wife and me, with our brood,
teaching my sons and my daughters
to fish for perch from the rails,
watching them feed flocking seagulls

with crumbs of old bread.

And at the sundown end of every humid summer day,
with nothing else moving,
and the lake flat as a silent mirror that tells no lies,
we'd all sit side by side on a wooden bench,
feet propped up on the rails,
watching the shore lights twinkle on,
so near and yet so far away,
wishing the whole town well,
and sweet dreams and easy rest,
as the rippled river surge lapped against the piers.

On whitecap days, entering freighters hooted greetings.
And laundry flapped from clotheslines rigged to a boat davit.

On nights of deep fog rolling,
the horns would harrumph their calls,
and my kids would sit quiet with my wife and me,
their night shirts bunched against the chill,
mouths agape and watching the thick of things together.
Out of the mist a ship would suddenly loom, close enough
to be reached out to and almost touched.
And a voice from the bridge asking: "This is the port of Lorain?"
"Yep, it is."
"Thank God." And the sigh of the crew at the news.

When storms came in, I'd struggle from window to window,
figuring which steel shutters need closing for safety.
Then I'd go inside, pull the big steel door shut.
I'd build a fire in the fireplace.
Smoke would rise up the chimney.
We'd sing songs and pop corn.
Marshmallows would be brought out.

Before I went to bed, I'd haul up to the lantern tower
and double check the Fresnel beam,
just in case there were ships out there, about to be lost at sea.
Then we'd all go to sleep
and never have to worry the scream of the wind
or the crash of the water.

When morning came the lake would be calming out,
like a wrinkled sheet that somebody was about to iron.
Bacon would be frying, with smell of toast,
and the town would still be there, always,
just the way I'd left it, before all the storms began.

LAKEVIEW PARK

Along that stretch of meager beach and
low bluff of shading trees, there was (still is)
Lorain's big show-park where the town fathers
pulled out all the stops to make it fancy.

A brown field cannon from some former war,
with kids climbing it and cranking all the cranks,
and a gray anchor lying on its side,
cocked by its shank into jaunty stance,
so big it would have sunk lesser ships
that might have tried to carry it, and
a woven basket, brightly painted and big enough for giants,
that just before Easter every year a crew of city workers
installs with huge and multi-colored eggs
cast from concrete.

A square and solid summer pavilion built to survive tornadoes,
with changing rooms and showers,
and swinging screen doors, and refreshments for sale
to quench your thirst on summer-sandy barefoot days.

And a fountain gurgles and surges in midst of stones by day
but after dark on summer nights it geysers skyward
in huge pressured streams that fan out with bursts of spray,
and colored lights play on it, garnering pleasured gasps of
onlookers.

In the deeper night, and the rest of the town safe at home,
carloads of ardent lovers creep quietly into the nether ends
of the parking lot, pulling up to their own separate stops,
and slowly steaming their windows.

Circling beds of new flowers, laced criss-cross with walkways,
wending through crocuses and daffodils, tulips and pansies

and rosebushes, of course, in healthy abundance.

A golf-like green of cross-cut lawn
that old men in sporty trousers and white shirts
with long sleeves turned up, would roll balls across,
in the dimming-dwindling light of summer days,
playing slow-silent games to rules that
most onlookers never would understand.

In winter the stormy lake would gobble up the beach.
The bath house would be shuttered tight,
ready for any storm that might come its way.
The flowers would have long ago died and blown flat.
The trees, blown bare, would bend as the wind slanted in
as it always did, blown by the lake's anger.
The fountain would be drained and sealed shut,
and the huge Easter eggs long gone from their baskets.

In the deeper night, and the rest of the town safe at home,
carloads of ardent lovers creep quietly into the nether ends
of the parking lot, pulling up to their own separate stops,
and slowly steaming their windows.

LAKE THAT CARVED OHIO

Dark and brooding northern top of Lorain,
that slashes shorelines into place
whatever way it wants them –

Lake that carves Ohio's upper border
and sweeps around, forming
distances of south-water Canada --

Bright-day-sparkling lake in breezy sunshine
makes the town feel sootless and fancy free,
as if it somehow sees itself in a vast mirror
that always hides its flaws.

Lake that when cloud layers keep the sun at bay,
only magnifies gray atmospheres in its reflected surface
and makes the town seem forced
to play the old and white-powdered man
in the high school play --

Lake that lashes out to storm shorelines
and seethes rage in its shallow basin,
making everybody scurry for safe harbor,
away from the winds –

Lake that is so much a part of what I remember as Lorain --

Back in a time a long time ago, the fish began to die
from poison the factories dumped in the water,
and death rolled itself up onto beaches in the surge,
perch and catfish, sheephead, scaly carp,
white bass, and even big pickerel and walleye from deep water.

White-fleshed heaps of fish corpses lying there silent,
becoming eyeless – some say it was the seagulls

pecked out the eyes.
Whatever it was, there they'd lay in
empty-socketed bodies, bloating,
and on humid nights when the wind was still,
the whole town would begin to smell like an evil chowder.

People said the lake itself was dying,
and the gray water wasn't just on sunless days,
it was every day,
and one by one the twinkling lights
of the night fishermen
began to disappear,
until the midnight lake was black-dark
and everybody began to think
there was nothing left to do
except give up.

But the lake didn't die.
Finally somebody somewhere
figured out the thing to do
was to stop the piped-in poison factory junk
and not take no for an answer.
So they made the culprits all around the lake
begin to clean up their acts.
And that was that.

After a while, the fish learned it was safe to return,
and the factories went back to figuring out
how to keep making money anyway, even if
sometimes that meant moving out of town.

So that now, on certain bright days,
the Lake sparkles again, blue and bright green
and only gray in the gloom,
and lights of the night fishermen shine again
like stars in the dark water.

Oh the Lake still rages when storms blow,
but it's a cleaner kind of rage now,
the way it used to be in the best of days.

And for some huckleberry-tom-sawyer kids,
the Lake is again become the Mississippi itself,
inviting escape in small boats and outboard motors
to far off islands beyond horizons,
Middle Bass, Put-in-Bay and even Pelee,
and a tropical beach at Kelly's that
no one ever came to,
except boys in olden days, with cigars,
ready to sleep beneath the stars
and never go home.

TORNADO

When I am born the Big Tornado
is only eighteen years ago.
People still talk of it with tears that fill their eyes,
and their voices are hushed with awe,
as if that terrible storm was yesterday.

The big tree at the edge of the alley survived,
even though the roof blew off the garage
and crushed the Buick.

The honeysuckle trellis tumbled over but didn't break,
and the vines just continued to thrive
as if nothing ever had happened.

But children perished in the State Theater matinee,
and everyone, it seems, remembers the name and smile
of at least one of them who was lost.

When I am born, those perished children
would be old enough, almosg, to be
bearing playmates I'll never have.

CITY OF PORCHES (A dozen variations)

Once upon a time the Steel City lived on its porches,
back before TV, back before
the inside summer air of houses
got to be air-conditioned.
Drive down any street of older homes,
and there they are, standing proud
and pressing out into the green lawns,
full of their own stories –
of heat waves or thunder storms,
of quiet times at the end of days,
of golden autumns, or grief, or holidays.

1

Old men and young men in white-vested undershirts
would sit, silent, elbows resting
on curving-tubed arms of metal chairs,
fingers laced across their bellies,
gazing out their last leisure moments
and trying to put the Mill away from their minds
until time for the next shift.

2

Walk down any street in summer darkness
and hear the radio ballgame, hum of the crowd sound
behind hesitating voices of sports announcers
in spaces between plays,
and every so often the clack of a ball
clobbered by a bat,
and the roar from the stands.
All is well, the sound says,
all is as it has been.
And whether the Cleveland Indians
win or lose tonight, all is as it should be.

3
Mandolins brought from the old country
would be plucked on porches
in that same darkness,
on nights when the Tribe played away,
and the music sounded into the night
until time to go upstairs and settle into sleep.

4
Loves would begin in darkness of porches
on breezeless evenings
nestled close upon the wooden slats of wide swings,
hung by spring-ed chains from wooden ceilings,
and the swings creaked
and the neighbors would hear,
so the lovers would learn to sit silent and whisper,
dreaming into their futures.

5
White-haired ladies and ancient men
would sit on painted rockers,
eyes closed, pondering sadness
or perhaps remembering intervals of joy --
joy that salted itself in among the turmoils
and the strife of the life that got them there.

6
On screened porches, shaded lamps
on rickety wicker tables
would cast a yellow glow for the reading of books
and sometimes even games of Parcheesi
and the dull rattle of dice jiggling in their cups.

7
Lightning in distances and thunder
would be marveled from porches, with *oohs*

and *ahhs* and "That was the biggest one so far!"
Downpours of pummeling rain would drench lawns,
as on-lookers from their silent rockers
basked in satisfaction of not having to water the flowers.

8

Heat waves were endured on porches
with palm fans and paper fans.
Smoky flickering citronella candles
in the buggy seasons.
Leisey's Light and lemonade,
P.O.C. swigged from its brown bottles
and *Kool-Aid* served in soft plastic tumblers,
each containing a single, misty cube of ice
while chairs rocked and gliders glided and swings swung
and silence often became the only word of the evening.

9

On Sundays, families escaped the stove heat
from pork roasts or chicken *paprikash* or
corned beef or fried chicken or *pirogis*
or boiling ears of corn.
After dinner, everybody kicked back,
some of them drowsing away the food,
or watching with half-closed eyelids,
the breeze unsettling the leaves of trees
and sometime later all of them rising
to eat ice cream or angel food cake.

10

Second-floor porches loomed mysterious
up above and sometimes yielded
sounds of snoring, on hottest nights
and even into autumn,
and at least one lonely man
lived out the quarantine of his tuberculosis up there

and lived to forget it.

11

Of course there were sometimes angry neighbors
shouting to neighbors on other porches,
standing like arms-folded monarchs
upon parapets, gesturing with fists.
Sometimes wives would be wailing
at absconding husbands fleeing
the heat of the moment,
but these were not the usual events
in the lives of porches.

12

On crisp Saturday afternoons of October,
after the leaves were raked,
the rakers would recline on porches,
watching more leaves begin to straggle down
from browning trees and blazing maples

In winters, of course, the porches would be dormant.
The screens from all the windows of the house
would stack against each other
after storm windows had been put up.
Pumpkin pies would be set to cool on the rails.
The cut Christmas tree would be
stored there, resting on its side
bristling green and pungent with promises of festivity.
And even in the bleakness of snow upon the porch rail
would be the memory of summer evenings
and dreams of warmer weather.

TRAINS GOING EVERYDAY SOMEWHERE

I used to watch the trains go everyday somewhere,
roaring through my town, without even slowing down.
At night I'd dream how they got to where they were going,
all dripping and heaving and ready to rest
in Chicago, New York even, everywhere --
and all of those places without me.

 And then one day, I flagged one down, climbed on,
-- and lost my dream -- gaining the world, of course --
or so I tell myself.

II. Industry that Was

IN THE GRAND OLD BLAST FURNACE DAYS

In the grand old blast furnace days,
the place'd be roaring constant,
smoke belching from every smokestack,
and 28th Street with all of its
beer-scented bars and saloons,
ready to welcome the end of a shift.

Clouds of smoke and white steam,
billowing up and angling into the sky,
like some devil-ship, locked solid into the land,
and at any hour of deep night was an orange glow
lighting up the darkness into twilight, all night –
the kind of glow that only visits the city of prosperity –
and only while it flourishes.

Thousands working 7-to-3, 3-to-11, 11-to-7
swing shifting with whistles blowing,
and sirens – yes, sometimes sirens,
and always factory-belch and groan,
hard work and no complaining,
or everybody complaining,
depends on who you listened to,
with seamless mills and the line for continuous weld
hungry always for fresh ingot,
and the blast furnaces eager to comply.

When the wind was right, on warm nights
would be this ripe smell of what people said
was like rotten eggs –
they called it Hell's aroma, and it was, and yet
when you closed your eyes on it, you could smile
– it was the smell of work going strong

and never going to let up, the smell released
from toil of leather-aproned heroes, perspiring
and standing back, shielding faces from bright glow
and flashing spark of new steel that was ladle-poured
and wrought just now before their eyes

-- almost ready to ship to the world.

SLAG MOUNTAIN

Whole families, and also lovers, no doubt,
would pull their cars off Henderson Drive
and park along the grassy shoulders,
just before the High-Level Bridge at sunset,
and when the sun was gone,
the orange glow of the night shift mill
was the only light to see by.

Across the way and up high -- the Slag Mountain,
building itself night after night beneath the wheels
and tracks of the rickety pusher train that crested it.

It was the train we came to see.

Kids, kneeling on back seats
and elbowing out of open car windows,
craning their necks for the first glimpse,
calling out in hoarse whispers: "There it is! It's coming!"
Slag-hopper cauldron cars in the lead,
followed by a single, weary engine
up the bleak hill that was slow-forming beneath itself
round a curve and squeaking,
each car the shape of an upside-down
tippable-swivel church bell
about to be rung by a separate devil.

Train lurching to a stop, just before the lead car
would have tumbled down the end of the line,
with screech of brakes the only sound,
steam rising from each silent cauldron,
everybody knowing that each car roiled and sloshed
with glowing contents not yet seen,
as shadows of men, not devils,
back-lit by dull and flickering orange light

from the groaning mills
climbed down and moved around,
to go about the slow business of making the mountain
from what was left by the steel.

Then, without fanfare, one by one,
each of the hoppers began to swivel on silent axis,
and tons of still-molten slag waste started spewing out
and pouring down the bank, red hot and splashing fire,
Lorain's own lava flows of Kilauea.

It was volcanoes every night.
It was fireworks.
And the people gasping in their cars, and cheering,
with little children in footed pajamas
or seersucker when the weather was hot,
roused from falling asleep,
so that innocent eyes opened wide
with new wonder at the ways of the world.

For finale, they bumped
the hopper swivels against their limits,
shaking loose the still-glowing crust forming within them,
and down the glowing cliff came cascading
red-heated chunks of new-formed stone,
sparks spraying upward, as if in celebration.

When it was done, the train chugged away,
back down the hill and into the mill.
One by one the headlights of cars would come on,
and everyone would drive away,
leaving the new part of the mountain
to cool into its new form.

Everyone going home to dream.

AT NIGHT, THE RIVER

At night, the river bristled in twinkle of light
and sharp ripple of black flickering water.
Tugs hurried, chugging out
to meet their freighters in the deep lake.
And the sand dredge, burdened down to its gunnels
with new sloppy sand for concrete
sloshed its way back up river.
The big knives of bridge would groan open, then closed.
Grinding ore docks motors whining and whirring.
Emptied hopper cars at the coal docks
being slammed back onto their wheels
and re-connected to their waiting trains.

And the yammering outboards
and rumbling inboard engines
of lap-straked Lyman Islanders
ferried their serious night fishermen
out and back from the pickerel banks.

BEAM LAUNCH OF THE WILFRED SYKES

At the first breath of dawning, the shipyard carpenters
chop away with big axes, each stroke carefully placed,
at final braces of wooden framework
that holds the new dry hull of the Wilfred Sykes
in the place where it's been fabricated,
up slope from the deep water it will be birthed into.

This is a lost art, now forgotten,
careful work of the highly skilled,
choreography of the sticks,
down to the final minimum,
so that when those are pulled away,
the whole ship will slide,
perfect and sideways into the river,
pushing out the first massive splash
that christens it.

And after the words are said
on the crackling public address,
down to the water goes the ship,
precisely as planned,
and the hull rolls and then rolls back
and pulls for the first time against its tethers
and comes to rest, silent and proud.
Crowds cheer from the river's other side.
The largest Great Lakes ore carrier, ever, is new born.
The level of all water rises to make room.

ORE DOCKS

On the Black River near the Erie Bridge
stood the ore docks and the iron-giant apparatus
that accomplished the unloading of the ships
down from Lake Superior.

Open jaws of cable-dropped buckets
biting into the hold of a moored lake freighter,
and from the force of the drop
they'd chew their way deep
into its brown-ore contents.
When buckets were full
and the teeth had clamped themselves shut,
the cables lifting -
big electric motors whirring -
as high as they could go.

Then gears of the loaders groaning and grinding
and all of the downtown, and
everybody crossing the bridge and all the way up
to Brendan Regan's Grocery on the other side
could hear the sound and feel that grinding
in their own teeth, in their shoulders,
and know that everything was proceeding according to plan
It was that groan and grind
that kept the town in on things down at the docks.

The buckets would dangle and swing themselves across
to hover above railroad tracks and the waiting hopper cars,
into which the ore was lowered.
Teeth of the buckets opened wide
and deposited their contents gracefully,
for transport down to hungering steel mills.
Emptied, the freighter would ballast off
and head back for Minnesota.

GYPSUM PLANT

One year they put up the Gypsum Plant,
big long corrugated shack of a place
up at where the River bends around
behind the High-Level Bridge not far from
where they used to dump the slag.

The place where they'd cook the drywall into being
from slurry batter sandwiched between
long streams of cardboard sheets taped at the edges
in one continuing process not as elegant as rolling steel -
wallboard-making didn't seem at first to have its heroes --
and the mud-slurry set up like concrete
as the line rolled down to the ovens
and afterward got sliced like flat
bread crackers for some kind of giant
who never got enough to eat.

And when the slurry-hopper clogged,
you climbed into a rubber suit
and face shield and then hacked away
with chipping tools at the mixer's blades
until the big rotor broke loose
and tossed up some kind of mudded burst
that covered everyone and
made all of you curse and laugh
all at the same time like little children almost,
and the rubber suit covered with white slime
that had to be hosed off in the back room.

With big Jimmy D across the rolling line,
white tee shirt barely covering his full belly,
spatula in hand and yacking all the time,
authority about everything,
shouting over sounds of the big steel rollers

giving advice nobody seemed to care about,
Jimmy D telling you they'd be
running asbestos on Saturday night,
"they always run that crap on Saturday"
only he didn't say 'crap,'
Jimmy D coming back from his lunch break,
saying "I'll take your shift on Saturday, kid.
You don't want to be around that stuff.
And don't even listen to 'em when they tell you
it won't hurt you cuz it *will* hurt you."

And without even objecting very much,
you let him take your shift.

STEEL PLANT TOUR

One year they had a steel plant tour for the whole town,
everybody finally released to discover what it was
that went on inside that long brown scar of industry
that broke the green of our city.

Chartered buses entering plant gates and rumbling
down the bumpy dusty road beside the railroad tracks
to the furnaces, the Seamless Mill,
and the new Continuous Weld Plant.
Buses filled with kids and wives of workers,
the whole town wearing hardhats and goggles,
heads bobbing and swaying like odd armies of insects,
they made their entrance more smoothly
than invasions into the territory of enemies.

Bussed in to watch their hero fathers and husbands
splash the molten ingots into molds,
or roll the sheet steel in the din of deafening noise
or form the seamless tube or shape and fuse the pipe.
It was just like that. It was magnificent!

Discovering and celebrating the beauty of the labor
that till then was only taken for granted.

BUT IT WASN'T ONLY THE STEEL

But it wasn't only steel
they made in Lorain, not by a far cry.

Only the steel could light up the landscape,
but in the shadows were the other places,
American Crucible, the Ford Plant
out beyond the edge of town,
going up in the hinter lands to assemble the Comets,
before they converted the lines for Econoline Vans

The Thew Shovel and White Roth, Nelson Stud Welding,
everybody working hard,
and only the sprawling Magic Chef oven factory
shut down and moved away.

Even sophisticated Lorain Products wires and plastic bases
that hid themselves in people's telephones
and accomplished fantastic things
that seem so simple you wouldn't even think about them,
like whatever it was that switched inside a called phone
to make it begin to ring.
Without Lorain, telephones would never have rung!

III. Sundry Places

FIRST CONGREGATIONAL CHURCH

Old church crushed flat by that
same tornado that killed the theater kids.
And out of its rubble rose the square-cube red brick structure
that, but for the white steeple crafted into the side of it
(a sort of reverent afterthought)
wouldn't even seem to be a church at all.
First Congregational became the United Church of Christ –
don't ask me why, I only went there because I had to,
in the early years, and never paid attention to theology.

But on one Sunday morning in July, windows open
and green leaves on trees waving in lake breezes
and beckoning through those tall accumulations
of clear glass-panes the Pilgrims were famous for –
on that one Sunday morning,
shoulder-to-shoulder in pew-cool quiet
when silent prayer had muffled the place
just before the organ cranked up to boom its intro
for the sermon hymn -- was my first and sudden clarity
that something might indeed exist beyond the world . . .

THE TRAIN STATION

The train station was a festive place
when the passenger trains came in.
People approached a trip on a train
the way devout Christians approach a cathedral,
with new ecstasy flowing in their veins.
The Nickel Plate sent four passenger trains a day
through Lorain, morning and evening east,
and morning and evening west.

You could sit upon the splintered wooden bed of that
steel-wheeled baggage cart they used for hauling
trunks and cases down off the baggage car,
waiting for the wobbled headlight
and the warble-sound of slow horn
from the silver and blue diesel engine
bending the train past
the old Stove Works to the west
or inching across the Black River bridge to the east.

Bells would clang and gates would lower
to stop the Broadway traffic,
red lights flashing as the train shuddered to a stop,
steam from brakes rising beside each
glistening silver coach and Pullman car.

Passengers would climb the slow steely steps
while black-suited conductors
were standing on the pavement
carefully studying their watches.
Loved ones on the station platform
would wave through big windows
and watch the passengers
as they stowed leather suitcases
and settled into seats.

Then doors would clang shut,
and the diesel engines would rev,
brakes would steam and release,
and the great train would creak and lurch
forward into a slow exit from the scene.

The Broadway traffic gates clanged open,
and that dwindling red light
that was hung from the end coach
would swing and disappear into distances
of a thousand possibilities.

BROADWAY BUILDING

The Broadway building was the downtown skyline:
four tall bustling stories
at the corner of the Loop
and looking out and over the River.

White marble walls inside, and slightly musty smell.
An elevator with tired white-gloved operator
and sliding metal folding gate
carried you up to the top floor,
where typewriters were clacking
and business was going on
behind glass-windowed wooden doors,
and the future was just around the corner.

ANTLERS HOTEL

Way back in the postcard-days when visitors
would spin the wire racks in pharmacies
and at the register-end of marble soda fountain counters –
there weren't many images to be found --
a couple of obvious ones from Lakeview Park
(the fountain and the bath house),
one that showed the lighthouse on a sunny white-capped day,
one that showed the coal dock ramp,
and then, oddly enough, always a postcard of the Antlers Hotel
at the edge of Washington Park,
sparkling new and squat and square on a summer's day and
just waiting for dignified guests to arrive --
in limousines -- from Cleveland.

Across the front and snug between the wings
the big sitting porch stretched, low green awning,
shading it down to darkness.
Who was it that in those deep shadows
behind railed flower boxes blooming
sat and rocked and watched the town go by,
watched the boy go by as he for the first time
contemplated what it might mean to a life
to be staying for nights at a time in such a place?

In later years, the boy, grown-to-teen,
with white carnation lapelled to his bow-tie dinner jacket
like a badge of some kind of passage,
would accompany girls in puffy formal dresses
and convenient wrist corsages
(that didn't have to be pinned by awkward fingers perspiring)
up the steps and past the porch and into that
Grand and mysterious Ballroom --
where he would learn at last to dance.

THE CIVIL DEFENSE TOWER

Remember the Civil Defense tower
that rose, white and square and slant roofed
high above the city, on metal stilts that started
in the shadow of the old City Hall?
Its own siren could wake you out of a winter sleep
from deep in a feather bed.
Life was so less complicated then,
when dangers had the grace to announce themselves
by line of sight.

After they figured out that Japanese
and German war planes wouldn't be coming in the night,
as once had been feared,
what did we need the tower for?

What is it they were watching for up there?
Russians? For a while it was Russians,
but they never came.
A Naval assault from Canada
in fast boats flying ferocious Maple Leaf flags?
The return of another funnel cloud?
A tell-tale glow in the Western Sky
that would signify the sacking of Sandusky?
Or perhaps the tiny, constant movement of
columns of sinister troops
that had just surprised Vermilion
and taken it without a fight
and now was marching on our outskirts
or forming battle lines and preparing
to cannonade our parapets?
Nobody ever seemed courageous enough
to be asking these questions way back then.
We just kept listening for the siren
and wondering what we'd do.

This next poem isn't going to make much sense at all to anyone who wasn't there way back when. It's a real inside poem – full of the names of notable folks who shouldn't be forgotten, ever, but you had to know them to remember them. So, if it turns out you're too young to be getting much out of this poem beyond the exuberance of my own memory, put it aside and read it to your grandparents later. Their eyes will light up when they remember --

THE HIGH SCHOOL

Ours was the only high school in town
except of course the nearby one for the super Catholics,
and we never really knew what they were up to.
Oh and yes, except for way-out-at-the-edge-of-town kids
who always had a Clearview of everything.
Admiral King was still just a hero of the
War that everyone was trying to forget,
and then there was a hole in the ground,
but you couldn't possibly imagine
it would ever become another school.
Who needed another school?

Lorain the Harbor High School.
The whole town just came together at its high school
like it always had, never thought about integration plans,
never thought about bussing, it just opened the doors wide,
and that was that. We were all together and happy about it.

Every kid from tough Central and South Lorain
blended with East Side and West Side kids.
white, so-called Anglo-Saxons, African-Americans.
Italian kids, Puerto Rican kids, and kids not more than
one generation away from every country in Eastern Europe:
Russia, Latvia, Lithuania, Estonia, Croatia, Slovenia, Serbia
Ukraine, Poland of course, Hungary and Czechoslovakia. . .

and they mixed up everybody together,
two to a locker and by the third week
nobody could remember where they were from,
until it was time at the end of the day to go back there,
to each separate neighborhood clustered in vicinity
of its own separate church or social club.
Everybody pronouncing the names of everybody else
the consonant combinations, the Latin - Italian softness,
the formally last name-first names
of some of the African Americans --
becoming second nature.

Noontime lunch room down the long
trophied hall beneath the auditorium,
noon movie upstairs, drop your coin in the battered metal box
bolted to the rail, and see the scratchy movie
flicker on a screen dotted with life saver candies.

Kids taking politics and the High Standard newspaper
and the Scimitar yearbook
far more seriously than they probably should have,
but they did, and we let them.

Cotton chemistry, Freshwater physics.
Joan Jameson slipped me novels to read, and poetry,
under my desk, like contraband or controlled substance.
(It wasn't exactly cool for a big guy to be reading novels
when he should have been playing football.
Joan Jameson knew the risks.)

Pete Smith in World History commanding everyone
to memorize a slogan that only got Its meaning
from the later leading of a life.

And Warren Rodgers, lover of words,
the great Advancer of writing, all kinds of writing,

coaxing the words out like sweat from an athlete,
rich words we might never have otherwise tried,
organizing those words into sense.
Before him there was only nonsense.

Lib Wright, Andy Rohrbaugh, Sheila Gethin
teaching how to talk important talk in front of groups.

Audra Smith stamping her foot and pounding her
passion for algebra, geometry and trig
into the heads of kids who started out
not even knowing what it was she was trying to say.

Amble down the wide corridor, lockers stacked on both sides.
I still remember the clicking combination
of the lock I shared with Waszily, across from C-11,
still can feel that gray lock swing open in my fingers.

Names of teachers I haven't even mentioned,
including my own U.S. History/ Home Ec mother
(speaking of *combinations*, she never quite knew
whether to cook something or chronicle it!)
And what is there that can be said in a single poem
for doing justice to characters like Aten,
characters like Drummond,
characters like Goehring?

Things got learned at LHS, even though
it was never really fashionable to admit it.
Football games got won, and as for basketball,
the stage auditorium wall got rolled away,
and there was the gym, stacking bleachers for games,
and for dances afterward in victory or defeat,
mirrored ball rotating for moody special effects with light
so that everyone got to forget where they were.

Music everywhere, every day five days a week
down corridor from physics and chem and
upstairs from the Auto Shop.
Pops Hansen's Choir and Freeman's Band and Orchestra,
even a little chorister group that featured the likes of
Father Guido Sarducci, before he even invented himself.
Where is there anymore music like that,
right in the midst of your life?

This is what we knew back then, we knew
that LHS would never end.
How could something so big and brick
and at the center of everything ever come to an end?
But it did come to an end, another hole in the ground.
All that's left is the looking back -
and the looking back has to be enough.

IV. War and Remembrance

THE UNION SOLDIER STATUE

Sad mustashioed Union Soldier gaunt with sacrifice
of endless war that never seems to daunt him,
butt of ancient rifle resting on the stone base that stands him,

all of him painted, dark navy blue of coat and cape and Kepi cap,
lighter blue of trouser and stripe, and fleshy pink tone of face,
glaring out with black blazing pupil of eye to keep the vigil.
His face might have been kind once but now has forgotten.

He used to stand atop a two-tiered fountain that
cascaded water down and cooled the air,
but then they moved him down
and penned him into the summer flowers of peace.

He sometimes frightened little children
by seeming always to be looking down on them,
with old men sitting on park benches reading newspapers,
and sometimes even his rifle would come up missing.

Guarding all of the bright and sun-dappled
green days of tulip trees and elm,
guarding dry-brown dropped leaves of Autumn,
crisping across the sandstone pavement
and swirling under his feet,
with new-shouldered robin for companion
in earliest Spring, or pigeons at least,

the sad Union Soldier in great blue coat
and flapping cape and jaunty Kepi
standing guard over Washington Park forever.

FLAG MAST AT THE NAVAL RESERVE

If you close your eyes, even now,
you can still imagine the flag mast
on the grounds of the Naval Reserve.
It stood beside the Quonset building and
down the street from Longfellow School.

You can still hear the halyard flapping against metal
while wind blows in from the Lake.
You can still see stars and stripes flying proud
and hear the signal halyards that stretched
from the wide yard arm -- vibrating like a harp.

And you can remember, if I remind you,
that it seemed always to hold its own kind of majesty,
as if, all by itself, it signified the blood of heroes.

What you probably didn't know,
because nobody bothered to tell you,
is that this very mast had been one of the
two top masts that stood above the
superstructure communications towers
on the USS Arizona when it took the first blows
of that surprise attack that ended the peace for all of us,
the ship that lies beneath the rippled waters of Pearl Harbor.

Crusty Admiral King himself must have
used his considerable clout
to score the mast for Lorain.
And then, once it was in place,
everyone seemed to forget about
its valiant past, and left it alone.
-- It being in the nature of the people of Lorain
never to want to make a *thing* of things,

even when they turn out to be big things.

You won't be able to see that mast in Lorain any more
because they torched it down and sold it for salvage
to a guy, for fifty bucks, or something like that,
and he carted it away.

Fortunately for history, the guy had the grace
to remember what should have been present
in all of our minds, always.
He shipped the mast to Arizona (the State),
and now it rises again and holds the flags
on the front grounds of their Phoenix Capitol,
where it gets the honor it always deserved.

HEROES OF THE TWO BRIDGES

Two brave men from Lorain
won Congressional Medals of Honor
in that last official World War, only two,
and lost their lives doing it.
A separate one of Lorain's two big bridges
names itself in their honor,
a shrine to each.
And now the only thing we have to do
is remember to remember.

Charles Berry's Bridge

The Bridge at Erie Avenue, that opens high
and stops traffic when ships are passing through
is Charles Berry's Bridge – who was hardly more than
a boy out of Clearview School when he joined the Marines,
and, battle-seasoned and nearing the war's end,
he had to choose in one single instant to finish his life
by falling onto an Iwo Jima hand grenade
to save the life of his friends,
The soul of him was blown straight to heaven
faster than anybody else could get there.

At battle's end, his friends rose,
stood solemn, and bowed forward over him
to honor that he sacrificed for them to continue to live.

Charles Berry's bones are buried out at Elmwood
but the spirit of him we all should remember
lives in the Bridge they gave his name to.

Whenever that bridge is up, and its
two massive halves are standing tall against the sky,
bowing slightly forward over the always flowing river,

we remember those bowing friends of Charles Berry,
and their tribute to him, becomes ours.

Lofton Henderson's Bridge

The big high level bridge is Lofton Henderson's bridge,
connecting Twenty-First Street to the East Side,
the one whose silvery girders we can see
in gentle glinting arch when the sun sets
over fields of Lorain, and the bridge soars
high above the peaceful ships that pass beneath it.

Heading squadrons of Dauntless bombers
and flying as high as he could,
Lofton Henderson tried to dive on the warships of Japan
and stop their Midway Island attack,
way back near the war's beginning
and only shortly after Pearl Harbor laid us all low.

And though he failed and his life was lost
in a ball of flame that pressed the attack to the very end,
he slowed them enough to turn the tide of battle.
Shot down with all his squadron,
he slammed into the strife-wracked ocean.

Imagine what might have been his final dream,
dream that would have taken Lofton Henderson
high above the ships below, in gentle glinting arch
as the sun sets on a long and busy day,
a gentle glinting arch over quiet fields of Lorain
and into a lasting peace.

*   *   *

Lorain has given a separate one of its bridges
to shrine each of these heroes,

and now the only thing we have to do
is remember to remember --
and in remembering, also to honor
all soldiers and sailors, airmen, Marines
who sacrificed life and comfort of body and mind
for people in freedom to continue
crossing bridges to get to where they need to be going.

V. Seasons

THE SUMMER CIRCUS COMES TO TOWN IN DEAD OF NIGHT

The summer circus comes to town in dead of night
on silver train sliding silent onto a siding.
Nobody speaks, as clusters of townspeople
try to find their way in the dark
and keep out from under foot.
Elephants on unison command pull the tents up,
while barrel-chested men in undershirts
pound stakes that guy thick ropes into place.

As day breaks the breakfast tent griddles hot cakes
and fries smoky bacon, so that all can eat –
those who've created the magical camp
of the Greatest Show on Earth,
right here in the back lot of Lakeview Park
beside the Nickel Plate tracks,
and those who this very night will play the clowns,
be shot from cannons, tame the lions,
and dazzle on trapeze and highest wire.

And the elephants, blinking their deep eyes
and swishing their gray tails,
wait to learn what it is they'll be asked to do next.

LAKE FLIES

People take to calling them Canadian Soldiers
because they come in from the lake
in thick swarms everywhere, silent, no buzzing,
and settle on porch screens and lighted store windows,
annoying the town by their simple massive existence.
Passive and flimsy winged,
skinny cylinders of bodies and two pronged tails,
who never seem to want a thing
except they hope to be left alone --
like the rest of us.
Even without the vacuum cleaner holocausts,
they all will die too soon.

OCTOBER LEAVES

October leaves of Lorain trees would flash
bright yellow and red and also crackle-brown
and flutter down to blanket lawns
and have to be swept into heaps
at the paved aprons of driveways
and than burned on still days –
with smoke meandering upward
in the low light quiet parts of the dwindling days.

And old men and young boys would go outside
with scraping rakes and packs of matches,
just for a chance to stand in the smoke
and breathe deeply.

It was the women who wanted
the blankets of leaves cleared from the lawns
and kept from blowing into nuisances.
The men didn't care about that;
they only loved to stand around and smell the smoke
-- and dream their visions.

Old men and young boys would stand
and let the air crispen around them
as the late sun disappeared on schedule,
earlier today than yesterday
and much earlier than last Saturday
when it still was Daylight Savings Time.
And in the darkening, the cores of burning leaf piles
would glow bright orange, like new-poured slag,
brightening faces of the old men and the young boys,
warming them, as they stood, leaning on rakes,
talking about the Browns and the Buckeyes,
telling tales about summer fish, contemplating autumn,
beginning to wonder what's for dinner.

SOMETIMES THE SNOW

Sometimes the snow, in full gray day
would be slanting past the scene
as a separate character,
bent upon its own separate mischief,
not noticing it was being watched
and not even caring that it was forming
into its own kind of beauty.

If it managed to slash itself under your visor
and onto your cheek, well then, you hated it,
especially in February or March,
after you'd already seen enough
of the stuff for one season.
And all you could think about
was the slush it was forming into,
beneath the sliding tires of your bicycle
down Cleveland Boulevard,
as you tried to make it home from school
without having to dismount
and walk along the sidewalk,
defeated again by the elements.

EASTER

Easter -- Lorain-style -- and long ago
church in the morning after breakfast perhaps
of hard boiled eggs cracked out of colored shells
that scatter on a saucer.

Between church and Easter dinner, the park.
Stroll gravelly paths among new flowers
and end up standing around that out-sized Easter basket,
oo-ing and *ahh-ing* the bigness of things.

Easter weather always iffy.
Sometimes the sky gray or heavy.
Daffodils bending, blown by the
bite of lake wind often laced with drizzle.
Watch crocuses wondering
whether this year, they've
arrived on scene too soon.

Girls and women and little kids --
all dressed like flowers.
Often, as if by miracle, sunshine
and the wind slackens, only for Easter Day
in a springtime always hesitating to arrive.

Giant Easter basket centering the flower maze --
filled with eggs no man could ever lift alone,
each of them cast from fine concrete
and then painted pastels and placed
by sweating workers with overhead derrick,
lifted from an otherwise-nondescript city dump truck,
with always that reporter from the Journal
snapping the photo to remind the town.

The father in the Army uniform stooping down

to bended knee and almost whispering to ask his kid
how he thinks those great big eggs
got up there into that basket,
and the boy exploding into his own whimsy:
"It must have been King Kong!"
(his arms opening wide
and reaching up at the sky as if
to offer the beast a welcoming embrace.)

Setting everyone to laughing
and agreeing this is the way
it must have happened.

Dinner sometime after mid-day,
ham or lamb and after dinner,
knife-sawn slices of a fat candy egg
bought for the family from the chocolate store
(-- it was Faroh's then.)

Finally everybody, now over-eaten
settling in to the annual replay
of that fading silent movie
on a flickering TV,
King of Kings,
showing Jesus shouldering a cross
and struggling up that final hill –
filling the whole family's eyes with tears.

VI. Eateries

CHOCOLATE SODAS

One chocolate soda, one for me, and then one for him –
at Peoples Drug Store on Broadway,
Saturday night in that bright streetlight
that made everything shiny.
My Dad and me, the two of us.

Bald pharmacist in white jacket
comes down from his medicine throne
and mixes the concoctions himself,
behind a marble-topped counter.
Smiling and bantering as he does.

Two big white paper cones jammed
into shiny metal bases,
water bubbling into the dollops of
cream that went in first,
and a pumped squirt of that thick brown syrup.

Long spoon stirring the final pushed-back jet
fizzing up chocolate bubbled froth
as my eyes dazzle.

To that moment I haven't known soda water.
Now my dad is introducing me,
talking about Brooklyn and egg creams and
me being ready for big-boy drinks.
A coming of age -- making me feel as if
we're two gents at a downtown saloon.

I drink it fast from a thick straw,
loving the way the bubbles stay and rise
above the level of the paper cones --

certain my cup has truly runneth over at last.

and the chocolate soda drops dripping
onto the marble counter.
I drink it fast but suddenly it's gone even faster
when bubbles collapse on themselves.

My father beside me on his curlicue, wire-backed stool,
spooning small vanilla bites of ice cream
and squeezing the frozen stuff
between his tongue and the roof of his mouth,
not chewing, waving his spoon and reminding me
I shouldn't eat mine too fast.

I remember even the ending, tipping the cone up
grasping the cold steel base,
the rich taste of that sweet final drop.

It was over so fast.
It tasted so good!

SUTTER'S RESTAURANT

Aroma of the fresh roasted nuts
wafting out the vents onto Broadway
and across the street to where the other Sutter's was.
Red pistachios and white, heaped onto trays
and cashews glistening still with oil,
waiting to be silver-scooped
into flat white bags
and taken to the movies.

After the movie, milkshakes in tall glass,
in table booths or at counter stools,
juke boxes, naugahyde everywhere,
and Mary runs the place and sometimes
she herself will take your order, smiling
as if she really isn't serious, but she is.
And sometimes John Sutter himself
is in the back, pressing hamburgers,
griddling them brown and checking the oil for the fries.

And when John Sutter sits at your table
he tells about the hard old days of twenty years before.
He points to the ketchup bottles along the counter
and saucers of cellophaned saltines,
tells you how for a penny or two
or for nothing at all
he'd fill a soup bowl with boiling water,
and a hungry person could prepare his own dinner:
tomato soup and crackers
and then go home happy.

Sutter's is always a place
you go home happy from.

FISH FRY AT THE MOOSE HALL

Summer Fridays the Moose Hall on Broadway
would be deep-frying whole pickerel,
fresh off the fishing boats docked in the river –
would serve the pickerel on paper plates,
with copious tartar sauce
-- french fries and cole slaw.

People would sit on folding wooden chairs
at long tables covered with white paper,
sipping new-tapped beer in frosted glasses
from the bar, marveling at the bounty,

while my Uncle Harold
in short-sleeved dress shirt and bolo tie
sat silent, as he always did,
picking over the bones,
and only nodding for a moment
with unsmiling face
to someone down the line
who'd be saying to him
didn't this taste even better
than lobster?

HEILMAN'S RESTAURANT

Until they changed Heilman's Restaurant
into something they thought was "colonial" --
cute lighted cupola up there on the roof,
and earth tones and printed wallpaper –
until they changed Heilman's Restaurant,
the place was just exactly like a ship inside,
dark blues everywhere, like the deep sea,
with brass portholes on swinging kitchen doors
and fake ports, up on a faux deck, white-lighted inside
as if there might indeed be a captain and a navigator
up there behind the wheelhouse, sitting down
to plot tomorrow's course to somewhere,
and making it seem that you were eating your meal
on the deck of a liner that was
making its way on a voyage-important.

Thick-stranded ropes up gangways and
fastened along perimeters and edges of things.
And hovering over everything, an upper deck,
with a lifeboat, covered in canvas,
and beyond that, an oil painting mural of sea and sky.

It didn't matter that you ordered southern fried chicken
or that it got presented in waxy paper
nestled in green plastic lattice basket,
or that the cream cole slaw, made with real whipping cream
was, according to your mother,
what made the restaurant world famous.

After dinner, a treasure chest
on the floor across from the cash register
where children who behaved
and ate their green peas mixed into their mashed potatoes
would be rewarded with opportunity to choose

one precious gift which, if one selected well,
might even be one of those braided finger traps
that when you tried to pull away, would always
grip onto you and not let your fingers go.

MR. GOULD'S CORNER STORE

Long before 7-11's was Mr. Gould's corner store
on Washington, diagonal from the High School.
No sign on outside red bricks, but everybody always
knew to call it *"Mr. Gould's."*

Always dark, without even fluorescents, only a couple of
single-bulbed globes, hanging down from the high ceiling
and linoleum laid over wood slats,
with frail Mr. Gould always there,
standing, a little unsteady, behind his counter.

Candy in front and reachable:
Hershey's and even *Mounds Bars*
and packages of two cup cakes,
some of them chocolate frosted,
some of them pink-marshmallowed
and covered with coconut, looking like snow-balls,
and penny candies and even those waxy things
that when you bit off their tops
you could gulp down a few drops of a sugary liquid,
and then you could chew the wax
until it made your jaw tired
and you had to spit it out.

Brown long sticks of salted pretzel, dry and hard,
in a glass jar with red metal top,
and Mr. Gould would grab the glass knob
and pop it open and hand you one
if you gave him a penny.

There must have been other things for sale there:
scouring pads, *Cheerios,* packages of clothespins,
pine-scented cleaning soaps, perhaps,
but children never noticed,

what with a tall cooler at the back of the store,
steel and glass, where the cold pop
was stacked on wooden slats
and you got to open the doors yourself
with big clicking handles, to make a choice.
Hires Rootbeer and *Vernors Ginger Ale*
and *Canada Dry,* but the *Vernors* was yellower
and prickled your nose when you sipped it,
and everybody liked it better. Then of course,
the prized *Grapette,* stacked in smaller six packs,
sweet and deep purple, capped in clear glass bottles
five cents; five cents for a full bottle of *Grapette,*
and Mr. Gould would pop the top for you
with an opener that was mounted on the wall
behind his cash drawer.
Ten ounces (or was it eight) just enough
to slake the thirst of a five year old
fresh off his tricycle.

VII. Some People

STANLEY DAVIES AT THE DAIRY QUEEN

Round-faced guy,
white waist apron folded high
so it didn't reach down his knees,
with close cropped hair,
and he always looked a little bit like
the Ore Boat sailor he once had been,
even though the Dairy Queen years were good to him.

No indoor seating at the Dairy Queen.
Square building, flat-topped,
whitest concrete blocks you've ever seen --
big windows in front got washed every morning
after the settled lake flies got vacuumed off.
You lined up at serving windows in front -
sweating the wait through hot-humid evenings,

Stanley Davies served only vanilla custard.
Ah, but what a *vanilla!* When people tasted it
they forgave him his meager menu.
They swore he had a secret formula. And he did.
The cone with the curl on top!
Flourish of wrist on the custard bulb, just so -
and there it was. Always nickel cones
for little kids, ten cents for bigger ones,
three-bulbed fifteen cent-ers for the hungry among us,
and for a quarter, you got a fist-sized giant
you could hardly finish.

You came away from Stanley Davies' Dairy Queen
feeling somehow blessed.
Even the milkshakes were consecrated.

Freezes were milkshakes without the milk
but spun with carbonated soda water instead,
No Cokes, only root beer - and *Vernors Ginger Ale*
trickled, fizzing from a chipped chrome tap,
alive in a waxed cup so it bubbled your nose -

Regular customers got nicknames -- no extra charge --
and usually yours fit you even better
than what your own mother had labeled you
all through your growing up.

On cold nights you could stand with Stanley Davies
for hours and talk philosophy.
He had a black bound book by Will and Ariel Durant
with tattered covers, that he kept on the painted shelf -
just below the drawer he kept the cash in.

"I can dip the cone in a chocolate topping for you.
It's good. It hardens like candy," he'd explain,
"but I don't serve a chocolate product."
That was the way he talked. *'A chocolate product.'*

The Dairy Queen itself is long gone now,
along with Stanley Davies.
There's no place left for school-bus-loads
of perspiring priests to stop, late on hot nights
to line up for milkshakes, the way they used to do.
And there's never really time anymore,
just to be standing around -- talking philosophy.
All the nicknames are forgotten.
Things have changed; they always do.

Rest in peace, Stanley Davies.
Beyond the world that's left to us
we still can savor the vanilla.
Beyond everything else, we still smile
when in the dark we hear you call our nicknames
and remember how things were.

LEARNING TO SWIM IN LORAIN

Louie Monis taught the whole town to swim,
one by one in the chlorine-steamy pool
down the long stairs
and through the sweaty dressing room
at the 28th Street YMCA.

Strong and serious aging walrus,
he'd show us the ways of the water,
then climb out and stand at the far end,
waiting for us to follow.

One by one and trembling, we clung to the gutter,
and studied, close up, the tiny square mosaic tiles
that lined the pool,
our faces grimacing with good intentions.
And at the *twee-eeet*! of Louie's whistle,
breathing deep and flailing, trying to remember
not to bend our knees as we kicked our feet,
we'd light out for the deep end, sixty feet away.
And *Minnow* status, then upwards to *Flying Fish,*
and beyond, on badges our mothers could sew
onto our bathing suits.
Without him, we'd all still be wearing
canvas covered air-bladder water wings
and standing by the shores of lakes and oceans of the world,
with only our toes in the water.

THE HIGH SCHOOL HIRES A NEW GUY

September of 1958 the caravan of cars
that circle the high school
searching for parking places
adds another car.
Forty-Nine Merc,
painted this perfect chartreuse color,
lowered and rumble-mufflered,
sweet sound – really sweet --
with something streaming from its
rear slanting antenna –
might have been a raccoon tail.

Guy in it was kind of slump shouldered
and gawkish, wearin' a Hawaiian shirt,
short sleeves rolled up just right
and leanin' forward over the wheel
like he owned the street. Cool!
"Who is that guy? Must be new," somebody said.

Car started pulling into the faculty lot.
"He can't go in there; that's for teachers."
"He *is* a teacher," said someone else.
"He is?"
"U.S. History."

Right then we were instantly sure
we'd finally learn the truth --
about everything
from the French and Indian Wars
to the Teapot Dome and beyond

For this one year anyway,
we'd learn something.

OUT AT THE OLD AIRPORT

Out at the old airport
piper cubs and occasional biplanes
tether in a shabby hangar
beside the runway's weeds and puddles.
The orange windsock tells you where the breeze is from.
Jess Freeman, the band master,
takes off and lands there, always into the wind,
on sunny Sundays, over and over.

And my uncle Tom Lyons, learning to fly,
once forgets about the windsock
and learns the hard way that airplanes
can even land upside down when they have to.
From the woods where he has run to hide,
he watches a reporter from the Journal
come out to take the picture.

WILD WEST

Once a year on a late August day
a thirsty quiet man in shirt sleeves and loosened tie,
jodhpur trousers and Hollywood-leather boots
would saunter down Washington Avenue
leading a saddled and sad-eyed pinto pony
with silver studded bridle, reins and martingale.
Saddle bags were filled with little chaps and cowboy hats
and fringed rawhide vests of different sizes.
And slung over the man's shoulder by a strap
was a square boxy camera;
its tripod had been fastened to the
pony's flank -- like the rifle of a gunslinger.

Door to door the man would go
and one by one the little children,
chapped and vested and hatted,
would be hoisted up onto the patient pony
for photos the mothers would pay for.

The man would adjust the stirrups
and show the children how to hold the reins.
Some of them of course, the littler ones,
would cry, but most would be dreaming
gallant dreams of thundering hooves
and jangling spurs and smiling cowboys,
shouting Yee-hah through the clouds of dust
their galloping made as they rode toward rescues.

"Now hold very still," the man would say.
The photos would flash, and the man would
stand the children down, dust them off
collect the borrowed garments
and move along down the street
with the sad-eyed pony swishing his tail.

Always, as promised, the mailman
of a late October morning would deliver
envelopes down the line, brown and over-sized,
and in them, images of a Romantic West,
starring, one-by-one, the smiling dreaming
children of Washington Avenue.

MILK WAGON

Milk wagon from the Creamery
down Washington Avenue.
Thick-footed Dolly the dray horse
plodding step by step and almost never stopping
but when she does you can reach up
and pet the stubble of her muzzled nose.

And the bottles clink in the wire metal carrier
as the milkman makes his way up and onto
every porch, to leave the new milk, cream rising,
and pick up the empties.

DUCK BLINDS

Duck blinds along the stone jetty out to the lighthouse.
Sagging wooden structures, cabled into the rocks
every couple hundred feet, where hunters would sit,
snug from the winter winds, sip whisky
and blast away at migrating birds,
making the flyway of Northern Ohio
extremely unsafe for feathers.

Until, in the stillness of one dark,
lakewater-lapping night,
late, after the summer lovers had left for home,
a small band of Robin Hood boys,
armed only with a single pair of cable cutters
borrowed from the metal shop
over at the high school,
proceeded slowly out the jetty,
duck blind to duck blind,
snapped each one of them free,
plopped them one by one into the slop
and watched them bob helplessly shoreward
to wreck themselves on the beach.

And the world, for a little while
got to be just a bit more welcoming for waterfowl.

VIII. Late Words

WHEN I WAS A BOY

When I was a boy, the town was a lot like it was,
back when the former century changed.
Fifty years of progress wasn't fully showing yet,
back before plastic took over the signs
and the cheaper fronts of stores.
Neon was king -- before fast food and franchise,
when milk and cheese and eggs and bread,
and of course newspapers morning and evening --
Lorain Journal, Cleveland Plain Dealer,
and even *The Cleveland News* --
were still delivered every day to people's doors.

Only one discount store, almost hidden somewhere,
as if it was a shame to be going there,
and the only mall in this part of the State
was just starting up. Nobody knew what to make of it,
back before anybody even thought to use the mall-word --
'Called it instead a shopping center and left it at that.

Hardware stores and pharmacies
named themselves after their owners, or places,
and always did their level best
to give *true value* and the *right aid*
without ever having to say so on signs.

Motels on the edges of town were few,
and they called them *motor lodges* or *cabins,*
your own clapboard building for the night.

They were quiet simple times.
Nobody seemed aware of what was coming.

77

When I say "you" in this next poem, what I'm hoping for is that you will put yourself in my shoes – back in a time before airplanes got to be as common as buses, back when they were still a little rare and exotic for a Lorain kid, six years old. Be that kid with me as you read this poem.

IT IS EARLY STILL AND YOU HAVE NEVER FLOWN

It is early still and you have never flown,
not over the gridded streets of Lorain,
not over heaven-pointing spires of churches,
not anywhere.

Of course you've seen airplanes,
but you've never been up to look down from one.
That will come later, but now, oh, you've been taken
on the long back-roads drive to Cleveland
and parked at the side of a dusty road
that runs along the Cyclone fenced airdrome perimeter.
And you've seen the flashing metal birds
drone in from the future and sputter their
awkward-graceful propeller landings,
backing their engines and making blue smoke,
wobbling back to balance on earth.

Flying still is only for movie stars and the idle rich,
and captains of the smoke-belch industries,
in their heavy woolen overcoats of Navy Blue.

And only weeks ago was the first you even learned
what a parachute must be,
when your new friend the first day you met him
fashioned a bed pillow, fastened to gallus-clasp suspenders,
and jumped from a high ledge in his house, and hurt his knee
and had to be taken down to St. Joseph's to be x-rayed.

But you have not yet flown above the streets of Lorain
and so have no idea how the parts of it
may link and come together;
that will be later. But now,
now you can only know it street by street,
sandstone sidewalk square by square,
some cracked, some new-quarried,
and some chisel-stamped with a brand name
and logo, that signals what is to come.

THE THINGS THAT MADE THE TOWN CLASSY

These are the things that made the town classy,
classy as any city anywhere,
significant as any green-treed capital in Europe:

The Broadway Building, where the future was,
and of course the elegant Antlers Hotel;

the Overlook Apartments
crusted in rough brown brick, and casement windows,
and that long green entrance awning across the sidewalk,
elegant as anything at Forest Hills in tennis season;

the swans at the Sanatorium ponds
when you visited them after Sunday School;

the three theaters downtown,
the *Palace*, where even the Ballet came one year
and dancing-toed feet thumped on the hollow stage;

the *Tivoli,* where once a year
they had the festival of foreign films,
and before that nobody in the town
even knew there was such a thing as a foreign film;

the *Ohio,* where The Eddie Duchin Story
showed us Tyrone Power and Kim Novak together
and what it meant for love, for a boy to dream
big city dreams -- and see them through;

Neisner's Five and Dime, just a cut above Kresge's up the street;

the store down Broadway that was always cool and dim
and sold tea leaves and coffee beans and fancy dishes

and rolling serving carts of polished walnut wood;

People's pharmacy with its marble soda counter;

The Waterworks, built out on the West Side
to resemble a kind of Ivy college campus;

And finally the way that apples
enough to feed the whole town all winter
got stored in that cooling locker out at the orchards --
because no city anywhere
ever had its own private stock of apples,
to see it through the hard times.

NOW HERE WE ARE

Now here we are, full formed,
out beyond the sperm and the egg
spark-forged in the dark,
and sprung into our own generation.
Looking back through the dim night
to the tiny lights of the place that spawned us.
Trying to find a pattern,
trying to see what it means.

Made in the USA
Columbia, SC
11 June 2019